THE BETTER VERSION
OF
YOURSELF

Place of publication: Oxford, United Kingdom.

Publishing company: Amazon Kindle

Author: Mihaela Piculist

Year of publication: 2021

All humans have the potential for doing both great good and great evil, it all depends on their choice. To choose to better yourself is to understand that the change you want to see in the world must be done by you.

SUMMARY

FOREWORD

Have you ever felt that no one can understand you? That despite your niceness and kindness people do not treat you as you want to be treated? If you answered yes to the first question your problem can still be solved, if you answer yes to both questions the change, you are looking for is almost impossible. To explicate what I mean by that is to tell you a little bit about, what Rotter (1954) termed "locus of control". Locus of control is the degree to which people believe that they, as opposed to external forces (beyond their reach), have control over the outcome of events in their lives. This locus of control exists as a trait of two extremes: internal locus of control and external locus of control. Individuals with a strong internal locus of control believe events in their life derive primarily from their own actions: for example, when receiving exam results, people with an internal locus of control tend to praise or blame themselves and their abilities. While people with a strong external locus of control tend to praise or blame external factors such as the teacher or the exam. If you answered with yes to both questions, to improve your life, you must switch the focus of who oversees your life.

We, as humans make mistakes all the time, we regret choices and often dwell in the past. The phrase "Carpe diem" that flies from the lips of many people, although translated as "seize the day" and not "live in the moment", is often misunderstood. The expression "Carpe diem", instead, invites each of us to be the best of ourselves in every given moment. Because what is the point of doing something if you are not giving your very best? So, what is the point of our existence if we are not striving to become the best we can possibly be? A tree left uncared for grows wild and will not bear fruit, same are we, should we not take care of our mind, should we not educate ourselves we would grow wild and bear no fruit. We would become a shadow in our own life and forgotten in our death. How to become our own best? By challenging ourselves, striving to become better with every new today, setting new goals to achieve, and keeping engaged with the world around us. This is the secret of a happy life. I hope this booklet will bring at least a little bit of light into your life.

I. THE MIND

The infant human does not spring into spring, like a baby deer but needs time to acquire skills and be able to use them. Humans do not spring into action immediately after birth, it takes longer to become active agents in their environments; this is because of the humans' excellent innate adaptability. Humans learn and challenge themselves continuously even before birth. Their learning progresses into becoming even more ferocious after their first breath.

This process is easier to understand if one looks at how babies learn. For example, in motor development, babies start by lifting their chin, twisting their body from one side to another, then sitting, crawling, walking, and running. Babies do not acquire all the necessary skills in one day; it takes time and continuous effort. It is important to mention, that like any living creature if human babies would have nothing to gain from learning to walk or to talk, no human being would be walking or talking today. Any living creature adapts and develops because of their environment; they will shape depending on how the environment treats them. For example, polar bears are white because it helps them hide in the snow, the dominant background in the northern hemisphere. The same is for humans, some humans have darker skin because they live in environments with high levels of sun exposure, they need extra melanin for protection against the strong ultraviolet rays of sunlight. Indeed, this psychical adaptation to the environment happened over centuries. However, unlike any living creature, humans can have thoughts and show motivation for their actions and are also able to intentionally self-actualise. For this reason, humans can change beyond biology.

The most straightforward way for a person to gain motivation in changing themselves is to focus on the gain the change will inevitably bring. Babies work hard at acquiring talking and walking because these skills facilitate their interactions with the social environment and similar others. These skills also aid their transition from extremely vulnerable and dependent beings to more independent individuals who begin to learn to defend themselves; those skills are a matter of survival for the species. Walking and talking represent skills that develop from the first weeks of life and become automated into adulthood. Walking and talking become so automated that a healthy person will convey no thought into how they can perform this. The same applies to many other skills practised to the level of automatization. You may now say that childhood had passed and is extremely difficult for you, now an adult, to acquire new skills, to learn, to become a better you. You may also say that learning is overly complicated, and that is too late to learn new skills. Indeed, two significant names from developmental psychology sustain your point; Piaget and Vygotsky argue that a critical period into humans' childhood when learning is easier does indeed exist. They say that once the critical time frame passes the ability to learn decreases drastically making learning up to tenfold more difficult into adulthood. These theories are briefly presented in Table 1.

Stage	Age Range	Areas of Development
Sensorimotor	0-2 years	Coordination of senses with motor responses. A sensory exploration of the world. Basic language development is used for asks and object recognition. Awareness of object

		permanence is also developed.
Pre-operational	2-7 years	Refining of language skills, such as using proper syntax and grammar as well as symbolic thinking. This stage is characterised by strong imagination and intuition; however, complex abstract thoughts are still difficult to grasp. Self-conservation is also developed.
Concrete Operational	7-11 years	Concepts attached to concrete situations. A general understanding and application of concepts such as time, space, and quantity can successfully be used.
Formal Operational	11 years and older	This stage is marked by extensive progress in refining the skills acquired in the

		previous stages. Theoretical, hypothetical, and counterfactual thinking, as well as abstract logic and reasoning, begin to be used by the child. Strategy and planning become possible as well as generalisation.

Table 1: Piaget's stage psycho-development in healthy children.

However, I argue that the end of this "critical period" is in fact not at all biological or even developmental, but rather social. *How would this be?* You might ask. I argue the "critical period" is in fact socially dependable because, with every step taken into the 'social world', the self begins to lose essential self-time required for self-improvement and self-actualisation. When this so-called "critical period" ends, is when distractions appear; distractions such as starting school, making friends, looking for a partner, building a career, creating a family, having children, etc. If you eliminate or successfully control all these 'distractors', the "sensitive period" returns, aid this with curiosity, a thirst for learning, and the anticipation of the end goal, and the learning process returns to its "critical period". By eliminating distractors or managing them in such a way that they do not drain out all the energy and time of the individual, it will allow more personal time to feed the intrinsic inquisitive nature that characterises every healthy child.

Curiosity is usually described as being a "childhood attribute", however, curiosity is not age dependent. Yet, it seems to drastically reduce even disappear into adulthood, right when life gets cramped with worries and commitments. *What am I saying with this?* Adeptly, I am trying to say that the mind has the same high potential for curiosity and learning at any given age and is not restricted by a "critical period". And despite Piaget's and Vygotsky's theories the "critical period" can be regained because the mind, here synonym with the brain, is like any muscle; it loses its edge if left untended to, but just like any muscle it can be 'revived' by a healthy diet and exercise regime. If left uncared for, the mind will lose its sharpness, because just like ceasing an intensive workout schedule, muscles that were once perky and firm lose their mass and elasticity. Fortunately, this 'perkiness' and 'sharpness' can be regained after returning to a healthy work-out schedule.

Returning to how a baby learns to walk and talk. Walking in two frees the child's hands allowing them to carry objects and interact with others, talking allows children to make demands and exchange information with other members of society. If there would have been other ways of facilitating these types of interactions essential for the maintenance of human society and even more, if these types of interactions would not be beneficial, even essential to humans, no human today would be walking and talking- at least according to Darwin. Darwin also argues that if at some point through the evolution of the human species this behaviour accidentally appeared holding no beneficial factor for the species, it would rapidly be extinguished, perhaps in a very few generations, because all behaviour costs energy. Every behaviour appears because of an intense need, and this is the secret behind gaining the motivation to learn anything. Sarah

Blakemore found the human brain fully matures at the age of 25, her results could explain why it is so laborious to learn complicated skills after the age of 25. But I argue that after the age of 25, a healthy mind will offer more control and better choice weighting. Perhaps the skills one struggles to acquire are seen as useless in a certain corner of the individual's mind. If the skills one tries to acquire is perceived as useless it will take forever to grasp it, or perhaps it would never be learned. The trick stands into finding the reality where the skill becomes of life and death importance. Yet, a sword that was left uncared for gathers rust and loses its edge, no matter what material it was forged from. To regain its edge the sword must be cleaned and sharpened. The same process applies to the human mind, the rust symbolises the distractions, harmful habits, and deficient diets. Sharpening the swords refers to the process of regaining the sharpness of the mind. How to train your brain? By exercising, by going to the actual gym or doing other types of physical exercise, because the mind needs a healthy combination of both physical exercise and mental exercise. The mind is both mass and circuits; it requires proper oxygenation, good blood circulation and a bit of mental flexing. Now, I am not saying to start solving the biggest quests like world hunger. I am suggesting starting with small steps, such as memorising a phone number, taking a different way home or to work, solving sudoku or a crossword puzzle. Sharpening the mind needs to start with easy steps which should facilitate the awakening of the inner child, the curiosity and thirst for knowledge. These small steps are eminently practical because they establish the basis for gaining necessary skills which will allow adding future layers on, even video gaming can be used for flexing the mind if it's not in an excessive amount.

In his bestseller "Games people play", Eric Berne highlights the fact that humans have three primary ego states, Eric Berne clearly presents them as Parent, Adult and Child ego states. His wording is easier than Freud's Ego, Id, and Superego. The most desirable ego state that every adult want is the Adult Ego State. But if left unchecked, the other Ego states can suddenly take over and overthrow the Ego-state left in charge, although that is barely possible to happen when the Ego-state in charge is the Child, that is because the Parent and the Adult would either be unformed or subdued by the Child. Throughout a lifetime, humans ordinarily first have the Child Ego state, or the Id argued to be innate with the primary function to preserve the individual. Belatedly, the Adult state appears, this is when the child is discovering their identity. And when the child is old enough, the Parent ego state surfaces, like an interiorized parent telling them that it is wrong to kick a dog, no matter how bad they want to do that. To keep all these Ego states in order and make sure there will not be any sudden inappropriate appearance of any other Ego state, a person must learn to give Caesar what belongs to Caesar. In this case, give each ego state what it demands. Creativity and curiosity belong to the Child, care and empathy for others belong to the Parent and responsibility and reliance to the Adult. All these ego states are important in making sure you are always your own best. Practice will make it easier to switch between Ego states when the situation requires it. Is basic; just three Ego states need manipulation to be the best version of yourself. But I would argue all you need is control over the Child ego state; capture the curiosity and thirst to learn and exploit them, exploit them by employing them every day. Be curious about the task ahead and be opened to assimilate what you need to. Curiosity will promote knowledge, learning will satisfy understanding, and experience will bring power; the more you know the more powerful you are.

II. WHO DO YOU WANT TO BE?

- Are you listening to yourself? -

"Give me a dozen healthy infants, well-formed, and my own specified world to bring them up in and I'll guarantee to take anyone at random and train him to become any type of specialist I might select—doctor, lawyer, artist, merchant-chief and, yes, even beggar-man and thief, regardless of his talents, penchants, tendencies, abilities, vocations, and race of his ancestors." J. B. Watson (1930)

Talking about the best version of yourself, who do you want to be? What are you seeing yourself do and be if you eliminate all the limitations that restrict you from being who you want to be? And what stops you from achieving that? We were all once little children, driven by curiosity and carrying stars in our eyes. We pretended to be doctors or police officers or bank directors or chiefs. We invested hours constructing a pretend adult identity. But by the time we must decide on our career in life, this childhood dream seems to be nowhere to be found. *Who do you want to be?* Well, many would say, I want to be rich, have a hot partner, maybe children a satisfying job and be happy. But how can one achieve that? For someone being a doctor and having a partner that is their best friend checks all the boxes. For someone else, being an accountant and travelling through Europe for the company's clients checks all the boxes. For others, these scenarios may sound like their most dreadful nightmares. We are all different, and despite having the same primary needs, these higher needs cannot be satisfied in the same way. Humans have tremendous potential in growing into whomever they set their minds to become. Despite genetics' influence on one's intellect or the environment they grow in, they can still bend and overcome impediments. Researchers have explored these issues, and there are many cases documented to have manipulated the laws of nature by pure will. So, you would have no arguments saying your brain does not have the power, or the environment is too restrictive. As long as you want to become who you want to become your will should bring you the solution as long as you don't give up.

You may want to argue that making a change now, that aiming to improve yourself in this right moment is too late, but I will tell you again, there is never too late! The brain is a muscle, a muscle that demonstrates tremendous potential. Oh, and humans are also extremely adaptable. You may remember the first time you read aloud a sentence and caused you to feel like having to catch your breath, but after years of reading, reading became like your second nature. Same with many skills, such as riding a bike, driving, swimming, etc. There are certain skills that become so automatized that they turn into behaviours, instincts, and reflexes. These learning processes can even be intentionally reversed by inhibiting a certain response as a reaction to an unconditioned stimulus. Revisiting the question, who do you want to be? If you close your eyes now and imagine yourself 5, 10 years in the future, what are you doing? Try to answer the following questions (I have added answers to give you some guidance on what these questions refer to).

Question	Answer
What are you doing?	I am lying on the hot sand, in LA.

Are you happy?	I am the happiest I have ever been.
What is your profession?	I am a brain surgeon.
Do you have a family of your own?	Yes.
Where do you live?	I live in Vienna, Austria.

Now is your turn to write these questions down and answer them. You can write up as many questions as you feel like and go into as much detail as you can.

Question	Answer
What car do you drive?	I drive a silver Tesla.
How many children do you have?	One daughter.
What pet do you have?	No pet.

Given the freedom of imagination, go as abstract as possible as long as is humanly achievable. After writing down your fictional future, tailor it to a more realistic setup.

Question	Answer
What are you doing?	I am lying on a beach.
Are you happy?	Yes.
What is your profession?	I am a doctor.
Where do you live?	I live in Vienna.
Do you have a family of your own?	Yes.
What car do you drive?	An electric car.

After tailoring the answers to a personalised realist scenery, set the milestones you would need to achieve to reach your goals, according to the following example.

- To become a doctor, you need to have a PhD.
- To live in Vienna, you may need to speak German.
- To have a family of your own, you might need a partner.
- To drive a car, you need a driving licence, and perhaps the car.

These planned outcomes set as milestones will pave the path to reach your desired goals. Everyone's goals are distinct, but they all follow the same route, trial, failure, repeat and succeed. And if the plan fails, just amend the plan, not the goal. There is no such thing as a destiny waiting for us, which no matter what path we will take will steer us to the same destination. We are the tailors of our own destinies, every choice we are making directs us closer or farther away from the established goal. *"Who do you want to be?"* sounds like a simple question, but many can't answer this immediately, and it is only natural to be unable to do this because this question is as complex as asking *"What is the meaning of life?"*.

III. LIVING LIFE WELL

- learn to enjoy each living moment-

Life is ridiculously short to live it in misery an regret, although sometimes we might feel like we have no say in what life throws at us, our mind can alter how we perceive and how we react to difficult life events. If we chose to lament our misfortune, we would only see misfortune and would let happiness pass us by. We should aim to make every living moment a moment we do not regret. In positive psychology, living life well is defined by three essential aspects, self-actualisation, autotelic personality, and spirituality. Starting with Maslow's pyramid of needs, positive psychology focussed on fulfilling the psychological needs of the self. Maslow has classified human needs in two large categories; biological needs like the need for food or shelter and psychological needs such as the need to feel loved and appreciated. Thus, the need Maslow placed at the top of the pyramid (see figure 1 for Maslow's pyramid of needs), is of psychological nature. This need is acknowledged by the scholar as being the pinnacle of living life well, and according to Maslow, it can only be fulfilled when the biological needs are already met. This need, despite its basic characteristics, is of a dynamic nature, meaning that is continuously subjective to changes and, requires changes to deliver a consistent level of satisfaction.

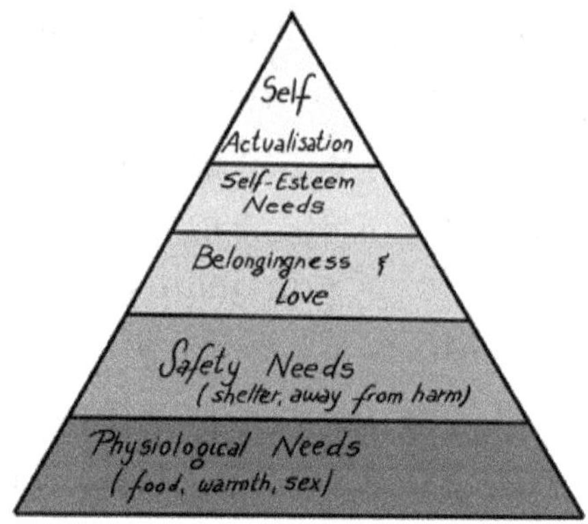

Figure 1:
Maslow's pyramid of needs.

Inspired by Maslow's pyramid of needs Csikszentmihalyi has explored the nature of self-actualisation in-depth and came with the concept of flow, a state which submerges the subject deep into their activity of preference blurring everything else out. This concept emerged after many interviews that Csikszentmihalyi conducted with skilled athletes, artists, musicians, and other experts. Csikszentmihalyi found anyone regardless of the level at which their needs are met can experience the phenomenon of flow if these three specific conditions are met; 1. The goals of what the activity requires the subject to do are clear and achievable, 2. There is a balance between the skills that the subject is equipped with and what the activity's requirements are, and 3. The activity provides instant feedback which helps guide the subject into maintaining a balance between their skills and the requirements of the activity. In his work, Csikszentmihalyi highlighted the positive outcomes experienced by the people who actively achieve flow. To better comprehend how the state of flow is different from other similar states, like unconsciousness, addiction, or other negative experiences, Csikszentmihalyi has identified six main characteristics of flow: 1. The subject must be fully engaged in the activity, allocating their full attention to the task at hand, 2. The subject must get immersed in the activity in such a way that they fail to acknowledge what happens around them. 3. The subject must be so immersed in the activity that they are completely living in the present moment, they are not ruminating on what happened during the day, and they do not worry about tomorrow while being engaged in the activity. 4. The participants must feel in charge of what happens during the activity and feel that they have control to choose what to do and when to do. 5. The participant perceives time flowing differently when they are experiencing flow, time either goes faster or slower, and 6. The subject experiences the activity as intrinsically rewarding. In one sentence, the participant engages in the activity simply because it causes them to feel good and not because of some external reward. What Csikszentmihalyi wants to say is that one can improve their overall wellbeing by seeking and engaging in activities that stimulate the onset of flow. Also, the scholar suggests that once you have mastered that skill and are no longer challenged by engaging in that activity, you can explore other activities. In Csikszentmihalyi's theory, the process of learning itself is what makes people experience flow- intense satisfaction. To such a degree, this is how the self-actualisation need, identified by Maslow can be effectively and continuously met. Although Csikszentmihalyi found a shortcut to reaching the pinnacle of Maslow's pyramid, a life truly lived well is when all steps from Maslow's pyramid are met. But in some cases, a need that's on a higher step can temporarily substitute for a previous need that is not fulfilled sufficiently.

However, even if those needs cannot completely be fulfilled, living life well is to choose to focus on the good things when in the worst situations and living happy is choosing to look at the proverbial glass as being half full, and not half empty. Intentionally choosing to focus on the positive side helps us maintain a general sense of happiness, reduces stress, and helps to solve problems faster. To live a life well, one must strive for balance. This balance extends to every single aspect of living. Because too much of a good thing is not good! No excess produces beneficial effects, even too much oxygen, the gas we are dependent on can kill us. Just like the Buddhism religion states about yin and yang, and that humans should situate themselves on the path between the two to achieve perfection. Living life well is to live in equilibrium with yourself.

Not to be forgotten, as living breathing beings our diet and lifestyle also play a fundamental role in our mental health, just like what the Latin proverb says "mens sana in corpore sana" which literally translates as "a sound mind in a healthy body". Diet, the sleep patterns we create, and how physically active we are, reflects into our minds; every so often when our minds are in chaos, putting our bodies in order can ripple into arranging our minds too. Even if we think we might never escape the mental health diagnosis that we might have gotten labelled with, a strict regime of keeping our minds and bodies in balance can at times rewrite the mental diagnosis we got labelled with, because our lives are driven by choice over anything else.

IV. ADDICTIVE BEHAVIOUR

<del>mind</del> *choice* over matter-

Addiction is the opposite of living life in equilibrium; addiction is the ingredient that turns balance into chaos and prevents life from returning to equilibrium. Addiction, many will argue, and rightfully so, is the worst illness of modern society. The word "addiction" will automatically make you think of illegal substances and drug abuse, but this is not exactly the case. Addiction is not limited to drug abuse; it is, unfortunately, more complex than that. The DSM-IV (APA; 2000) sets a few criteria to diagnose addiction - text found in the table below.

DSM-IV Substance Dependence Criteria
Addiction (termed substance dependence by the American Psychiatric Association) is defined as a maladaptive pattern of substance use leading to clinically significant impairment or distress, as manifested by three (or more) of the following, occurring any time in the same 12-month period: 1. Tolerance, as defined by either of the following: (a) A need for markedly increased amounts of the substance to achieve intoxication or the desired effect or

(b) Markedly diminished effect with continued use of the same amount of the substance.

2. Withdrawal, as manifested by either of the following:

(a) The characteristic withdrawal syndrome for the substance or

(b) The same (or closely related) substance is taken to relieve or avoid withdrawal symptoms.

3. The substance is often taken in larger amounts or over a longer period than intended.

4. There is a persistent desire or unsuccessful efforts to cut down or control substance use.

5. A great deal of time is spent in activities necessary to obtain the substance (such as visiting multiple doctors or driving long distances), use the substance (for example, chain-smoking) or recover from its effects.

6. Important social, occupational, or recreational activities are given up or reduced because of substance use.

7. The substance use is continued despite knowledge of having a persistent physical or psychological problem that is likely to have been caused or exacerbated by the substance (for example, current cocaine uses despite recognition of cocaine-induced depression or continued drinking despite recognition that an ulcer was made worse by alcohol consumption).

The DSM-IV criteria for substance dependence include several specifiers, one of which outlines whether substance dependence is with physiologic dependence (evidence of tolerance or withdrawal) or without physiologic dependence (no evidence of tolerance or withdrawal). In addition, remission categories are classified into four subtypes: (1) full, (2) early partial, (3) sustained, and (4) sustained partial; based on whether any of the criteria for abuse or dependence have been met and over what time frame. The remission category can also be used for patients receiving agonist therapy (such as methadone maintenance) or for those living in a controlled, drug-free environment.

Table 2. Addiction

Humans are by nature inclined to seek a purpose for their life, a reason for every action, and significance for every rainbow. When humans feel without purpose the hunger of the void pulls the individual into an abyss spiralling uncontrollably into a living Abyss. Humans often attempt to fill this void with drugs and alcohol that inevitably creates addiction. In the medical field, addiction is often described as being a disorder, a compulsive behaviour to consume the same substance or engage in the same activity, despite its harmful effects on the self and the ones around the addicted. Many scientists believe addiction is an incurable disease in which the addicted have no choice but to continue their behaviour, despite its harmful effects. From a biological point of view, these scientists can demonstrate their belief is right. The uniqueness of the biological organism is the one that traps 'powerless' humans into such disastrous situations. Those biological scientists believe an important role in addiction is the hereditary structure of the dopamine and serotonin receptors in one's brain, the critical role being played by the amount of dopamine, respective serotonin receptors that one inherits, this being the element that makes the difference between perceiving a drug as pleasurable or as harmful. On the environmental side of innate versus acquired, epigenetics explains that the genetic markers one inherits are at fault in addiction. Due to certain life experiences, the sensitive genetic markers which control addiction are switched on making the individual binge consuming an addictive drug after one single incidental use. These scientists argue that epigenetics account for the fact that addiction is a result of both innate and environmental factors. There are multiple reasons why a person would consume illicit substances, from involuntary to voluntary use; one may consume drugs out of curiosity, social or peer pressure, pleasure, or simply to numb an unbearable physical or psychological pain. But what is the reason for continuing to use the drugs, despite their harmful outcomes, and despite knowing that continuing using drugs is harmful for themselves and others, is still a question on all scientists' minds, with opinions split into two opposites parts; one that believes that biology is at fault, and the other one that believes the choice is made by the mind. Indeed, to break a behavioural habit is easier than to break a biological habit; therefore, believing that addiction is a psychological problem rather than a purely biological problem gives more chances of 'curing' the addicted. The mind has more power over the body than one can possibly imagine. One simple belief can completely alter us and the world around us.

The most abused substances in addiction today are nicotine, alcohol, and illicit drugs. The drugs that have psychoactive potency are the ones that create addiction, the more potent the drug is the more difficult is to stop using it. To break such an unpleasant habit, people need to possess a strong will, and they also must be prepared for the side effects that will trouble them in the absence of the psychoactive substance. There are many tried methods, from going cold turkey, to slowing down by using less of the addictive substance or to completely replacing the addictive substance with healthier or less illegal alternatives. You may have come across such things as non-alcoholic beers, decaffeinated coffee, and nicotine patches. These unusual items have not been created because someone was bored and decided to make them. These items have been created to support people cope with addiction and replace strong substances with less potent or less addictive options, such as replacing coffee with decaffeinated coffee, class A drugs with scripted methadone, cigarettes with nicotine patches, and alcoholic beer with alcohol-free beer. There is a diversity of techniques when it comes to 'healing' addiction, some are successful and some fail from the start. The most important thing is to do with the addict's attitude; they must recognise they have a problem; they must recognise they are addicted and must want to make the change. Otherwise, regardless of the quality of the rehabilitation service, the change will not happen.

It is also critical to keep in mind that a person who was once addicted to a certain substance will be tempted to consume it again, perhaps only hearing the word of the substance that made them addicted might switch on their craving. I do not know if you like chocolate, but assuming you do, as most people do. Imagine liking chocolate very much, only at the sight or sometimes only just hearing the word chocolate your mouth might begin salivating and your tongue will begin craving the delicious food. In line with this, there is a famous theory in psychology rooted in a biophysicist's curiosity.

Some readers might already recognize who I am referring to, some might not. His name is Ivan Pavlov. This reminded me of a pun that summarises his theory nicely, the pun goes like that: *"Q: Have you heard of Pavlov?" A: "Rings a bell."*. His theory goes by the terms of classical conditioning. This bio-physician wanted to record the quantity of saliva a dog produces while digesting food. He was only interested in investigating the digestive functions of the dogs, but luckily for psychology, he had discovered classical conditioning. Initially, Ivan Pavlov discovered that after a while the dogs began salivating at the sight of the white lab coats even before being served food. This, Pavlov concluded later, was because the dogs knew that the presence of the white lab coat would follow by food. Not long after, the dogs begin to salivate even earlier, as soon as the light of the room where they were kept would be switched on; the dogs would salivate at the expectation of food, with no food in sight. Observing such behaviour, Pavlov added an element that was not naturally associated with food, this was penned a neutral stimulus, this is the famous bell. See figure 2 for a short breakdown of the theory.

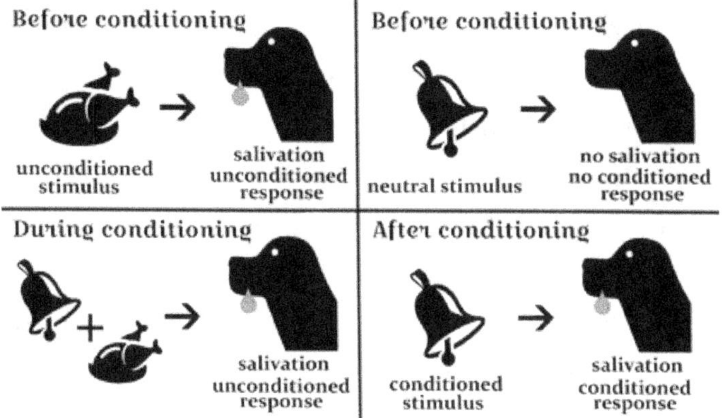

Figure 2: Classical conditioning.

Why am I talking about classical conditioning in relation to addiction? Because an option frequently used in breaking such behaviour is intentional conditioning by associating the usage of a certain drug with something negative or by reverse conditioning if the triggers are known. Reverse conditioning would work by dissociating the triggers from the addictive substance. Let's say that for a particular addict seeing a commercial for spirits will cause him to crave the alcohol, indeed this is the scope of the commercial. Knowing that watching a commercial for spirits make them crave the alcohol, the addict should instead of heading for the bottle of spirit do something else, the more opposite or displeasing the better, one such contrary stimulus could be eating a hot chilli pepper or drink a disgusting liquid such as, let's say pickle juice. Another type of therapy, heavily relying on classical conditioning, is cue exposure therapy. The cues, which in the dogs' case were the white lab coat, the switching on of the light and later the paired neutral stimulus; the bell, associated with the stimulus food are understood as conditioned stimuli. In substance addiction, the sights, smells, locations, people, and certain events become conditioned stimuli or triggers for the individual. With repeated cue exposure, and without engaging in addictive behaviour, these cues lose the power to induce the craving. Because most people in recovery cannot realistically eliminate every cue associated with their addiction, it becomes critical to reduce the power of these cues. This cue desensitisation can be achieved through therapy, through negative exposure practice (not acting upon the crave when around cues), and the passage of time. People who go through rehab but do not experience a reduction in the power of cues are at a higher risk of relapse.

It is worth mentioning that the most effective method of "healing" addiction is to replace it completely with some other "healthier" or less harmful addiction. It is known for a fact that many rehabilitation organisations were using this method in the past, replacing class A drugs with cigarettes. In the present illicit drugs are being replaced with methadone or buprenorphine, or other approved substitutes. To increase the success rate of the above-mentioned addiction treatments and ensure the treatment is lasting, professionals include talking therapies and/or CBT. There are a series of e-booklets to support people with reducing harm for alcohol and/or other substances of abuse; these are primarily provided by the NHS and Turning Point in the UK, and WHO and NICE Internationally. A simple search on any internet engine will present you with a series of choices. I remember when my dad gave up smoking, a habit he picked up while in the Army. He swore to himself that if his lips touched a cigarette again, the next animal poo he would see would become his food. My father owns a small farm, so I guess that aided him in his endeavour. After a while, he completely lost any craving for cigarettes and even began to find them disgusting. Some other people chew pens, candies, or snacks all the time to distract themselves from thinking about their addictions. Others switch one addiction for another or take prescribed medication. Not to sound self-promoting, but it is best that before one pursues the decision to break their addiction, they first consult with a psychologist, their family doctor, or other trained professionals, because going cold turkey with some addictions can lead to certain death due to severe withdrawal symptoms.

V. LEARNING and CREATIVITY
- Feeding the inner child-

Now, let us return to the primary purpose of this book; to teach you how to become a better version of yourself. The main process in becoming better than yesterday is to continue to learn. Learning is incredibly important, if a living creature is unable to learn, it will surely perish in the ever-changing environment we all live in. To survive, living creatures need to learn and adapt their behaviour in a continuous reciprocal relationship between their environment and themselves. Behaviourists have simply described behaviour, and even personality as a set of responses learned from the environment in a stimulus-response relationship. Here worth reminding you about Pavlov's dogs. Taking on Pavlov's work, Skinner suggested that humans learn not by associating certain stimuli with others but by reward and punishment. Skinner's theory makes sense to some extent, as is a more effective way of learning compared to classical conditioning. In contrast to Skinner's theory classical conditioning requires several repetitive pairings of the conditioned stimulus with the unconditioned stimulus for the desired response to be obtained. In Skinner's theory, reward or punishment can be effective as early as after the first trial, usually dependent on the intensity of the reward or punishment. Also, Skinner's conditioning benefits from more immunity in the extinction of the conditioned response. For example, getting an A+ for a biology exam might condition you to like the module, and show more interest in biology, a D- might condition you to hate the module and avert it at all costs. However, receiving a B would most likely not have an impact on the preference you show for the module. However, this example is limited, as grades are subjective, and have a subjective impact on individuals. A better example is touching something novel and burning yourself, you will learn, from only one trial that the novel object can hurt you. As a result, you will approach the same or similar situations more cautious at the next opportunity. Moreover, being paid for a job would condition you to perform that job again to obtain money if you are motivated by money. Skinner's theory suggests that in this way, humans and all living organisms learn throughout their evolution.

However, in the accounts of how humans learn, Bandura suggested a new theory, called a socio-cognitive theory. Bandura depicts a more optimistic picture of humankind; humans are not helpless individuals completely shaped by the environment, where they possess no freedom of choice like a rock falling that cannot choose to fall, does not decide to fall, it does not think about falling and does not consider different paths where it can fall. Bandura depicts humankind as active agents, that think, make decisions, and learn as active members of society, either by witnessing or experiencing. *Why do we learn?* Maslow, Ryan, Deci, Csikszentmihalyi, and many other humanistic scholars argue we learn because we strive to become the better version of ourselves. We naturally strive to improve ourselves and optimise the use of our environment. We are wired in such a way that when we fail, we work harder to succeed at the next opportunity. We also feel good when we achieve a goal, when we accomplish a task, or when we win. Because we feel good in these situations, we try reaching the same feeling again. This is largely the reason why we strive for self-improvement, why we are continuously learning and why we enjoy learning new things. Animals learn too; insects, bacteria, viruses; all biological things learn and adapt to their environments in a fight for survival. But as far as scientists have researched, humans are the ones that benefit the most from learning. Learning, for humankind, gave way to creativity. The simple theories of learning described by Pavlov, and Skinner is clearly observed in animals. However, humans seem to engage in more complex and exquisite learning behaviours; Bandura comprises, to some extent human learning behaviour through his socio-cognitive theory. However, Bandura's theory is insufficient.

Humans are stimulated so much by learning that they explore unique and novel ways of solving problems, this whole new process is known as creativity. Nonetheless, classical conditioning still works, this conditioning technique works better on whoever is unaware of being conditioned. Self-conditioning is trickier, but nonetheless effective, an excellent example is believing in superstitions. Beliefs that engage a certain behaviour which on its own will lead to the self-fulfilling of the superstition. However, learning is not always something people want to pursue, and often they need motivation, because the best way to learn something and to stick to its learning schedule is to be motivated. The Rogerians believed that people change their behaviour as a defence mechanism against complexes. For example, someone who was caught lying and became to be disrespected due to their lies will educate themselves in such a way that they will become champions of the truth, and perhaps will have careers in policing or law. Someone else, bullied as a child for their slip will grow to become a great orator with perfect diction, and perhaps build a career in public speaking. The Rogerians believe that people would be motivated to invest extra resources to compensate for their weaknesses when they perceive that the environment is punishing them for their shortcomings. Thus, according to Rogerians humans gain motivation to learn when trying to avoid punishment.

Another way to gain the motivation for learning is to understand your strengths and direct your resources towards enhancing these strengths. As agents of our own lives, we are the ones who should be able to identify our own strengths and weaknesses. However, despite being always in our own company, it is difficult to be objective and honest, our view will be biased by our feared self and our ideal self. Caught between the two of them, our answers may be far from reality. To counterbalance this, ask your close friends, family members, teachers; whoever you trust to give you honest answers to the following questions (the below table is an example).

WHAT IS MY BEST SKILL?
I am good at comforting people.
WHAT IS MY BEST QUALITY (of character)?
I am punctual.
HOW WOULD I DESCRIBE MYSELF IN ONE WORD (or sentence)?
Curious.
WHAT IS MY WORST SKILL (what am I the worst at)?
Socialising.

WHAT IS MY WORST QUALITY (of character)?
I rush a lot.
WHAT DO I THINK I NEED TO IMPROVE?
Social skills.
WHAT (behaviour/habit) OF WHAT I DO OFFENDS OTHERS?
Being too straight forward.
WHAT AM I BEING PRAISED FOR?
Creativity.
WHAT AM I BEING NAGGED FOR, and WHY?
Spending too much money because I buy things I do not need.

These questions serve as a quick basic investigation aimed at helping you identify the areas where you need to work on. Use the below table to identify your bests and worst qualities to use as your self-improvement goals. After answering these questions by yourself, ask your friends and family to do the same and see where the answers overlap. Once you got the answers create your self-improvement goals with them.

There is an old proverb saying that repetition is the master of learning; to learn something, you must repeat the process for as many times necessary. To learn to drive you must repeat numerous driving lessons, to learn to play the guitar, you must repeat lessons. However, there is a more efficient way of learning than repeating patterns of action into a habit. This easier method is by association, especially by associating the desired outcome or the process of learning with emotions. Such a process is often known as creativity and is another aspect of learning because creativity is facilitating learning. But what is Creativity? Most people associate creativity with the arts and not many would see creativity in maths or other less 'delicate' subjects. Research is still debating the nature of a truly creative act. However, a consensus on what constitutes a creative product exist, according to scientists and scholars a creative product is thought to be both novel and useful. But can a product truly be novel? As Isaac Newton says, "If I have seen further is because I am standing on the shoulders of giants" an idea is never truly original as an idea that is thought of in the present had most certainly also been thought of in the past. There are many cases where scientists from different corners of the world who did not know each other or had any contact with one another came to the same result and theories at the relatively same time. One example is the discoverers of the chemical neurotransmitter known under two names: orexin and hypocretin. Scientists argue that a truly creative product is one that is also useful. However, who can deny that Mona Lisa is not the result of a creative act? And yet, is Mona Lisa useful? Mona Lisa painting has little to no useful result but is known as a masterpiece of creativity. Furthermore, the process of coming up with ad-hoc pasta recipes is meeting the criteria for being a creative product, as it is both novel and useful, and yet there is a consensus that such a product cannot be called creative. Because of this dilemma, researchers have argued that a truly creative product is something that has an impact on humanity and remains in history— like something created by Mozart, the Beatles, da Vinci, or Einstein. To explain the confusion between creating a pasta recipe and coming up with the theory of relativity, researchers have divided creativity into two types of "C". Small c, which accounts for everyday creativity, such as coming up with a new recipe, making a new doodle while waiting for the train, discovering a face in a random stain. And Big C, which is describing the big genius minds that made an impact on humanity with their work.

Now, you might complain that you lack creativity and that simply put, you are uncreative. However, all humans are born creative. Creativity is described as thinking outside the box or thinking divergently by looking at the bigger picture. We see creativity in all young children, but by the time they are in elementary school, creativity seems to be quenched. This quenching in creativity is not a result of ageing, but unfortunately a result of the educational system and society which praises and rewards convergent thinking. As Pablo Picasso said, "we are all born creative, the challenge is in remaining creative into adulthood." The bright side is that we can still recover our creative potential into adulthood, by allowing ourselves to think outside the box, to come up with different ways of solving a problem, to experiment and to bring the joy of curiosity back into our lives. People often suppress their creative thinking because they are afraid of failing and are afraid of breaking norms. But today, society needs creative solutions. The most sought-after challenge is to find a solution for climate change, perhaps only by allowing ourselves to explore our creative potential, we might be able to save the planet. By achieving creativity, we achieve satisfaction in learning allowing ourselves to build a symbiotic process that improves our general wellbeing.

VI. HOW TO NOT CHANGE YOUR MIND

-Taking good decisions-

In life an unstable mind is one that cannot decide, and a person that is indecisive is perceived as unreliable, because nobody likes a flimsy person that changes their mind every second and cannot stick to one decision. This flimsiness can appear because of too many choices or the lack of self-confidence. If these two causes cannot be overcome, a simple strategy might bring the solution. This strategy requires exercise and determination, but its effectiveness is worthwhile. When you need to decide, choose the one that makes you feel less anxious, the one that you feel as being the easiest for you to fulfil and the one that you self-identify with even if its relativeness is of a small degree, and to reduce the chances of making the wrong choice follow the SWOT model (described in the picture below).

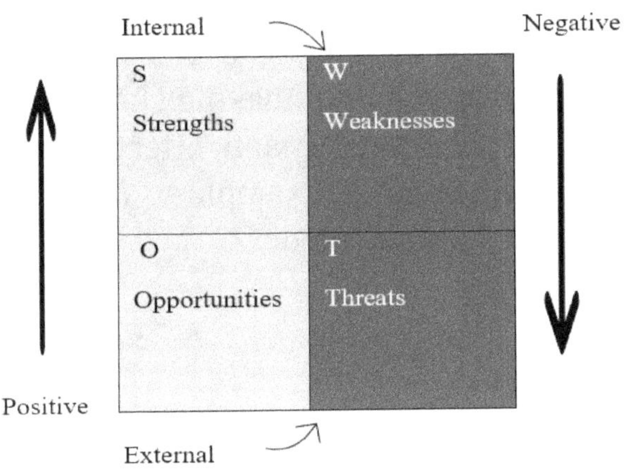

Figure 2. SWOT Analysis.

SWOT stands for Strengths, Weaknesses, Opportunities, and Threats. Strengths and weaknesses are internal, things that you have some control over and can change. Examples include skills you have, past experiences, means of realising your goal. Opportunities and threats are external, things that you cannot control. You can take advantage of opportunities and protect against threats, but you cannot change them. Examples include societal constraints, realistic aspects, previous successes realised by someone else. A SWOT analysis organises your top strengths, weaknesses, opportunities, and threats into an organised list and is usually presented in a simple two-by-two grid. SWOT is usually used in Business, Marketing, and Entrepreneurship, but it works very well in making choices in daily life too, as is a simple and effective method. Below is presented an example of a life choice, following the SWOT model.

Decision: *Choosing between an electric and a traditional car*

STRENGTHS/ GOOD POINTS	
TRADITIONAL: 1. Cheap to purchase 2. Easy access to fuel 3. Huge variety of options	ELECTRIC: 1. Environmentally friendly. 2. Cheaper in the long run. 3. Great options to choose from. 4. Paying less running and maintenance taxes. 5. Has a government grant.
WEAKNESSES/ BAD POINTS	
TRADITIONAL: 1. Polluting. 2. Expensive fuel. 3. Many running and maintenance taxes.	ELECTRIC: 1. Silent, therefore can be dangerous to pedestrians. 2. Expensive to own. 3. Not reliable for long-distance. 4. Takes very long to charge.

| | 5. No alternative if you run out of battery in the middle of nowhere.
6. Usually, batteries are purchased separately or are rented for an additional fee. |

OPPORTUNITIES

| TRADITIONAL:
1. Nothing new in terms of mechanics.
2. Exhausted market. | ELECTRIC:
1. Car of the future.
2. Opportunities for new development.
3. Technologically superior. |

THREATS

| TRADITIONAL:
1. Market threatened to come to an end, may become difficult to find pieces for the cars.
2. Risk of more taxes being introduced for owners of traditional cars. | ELECTRIC:
1. Developing market, with new and better models released month after month, which gives space to error. |

Final decision: SWOT scores

| Strengths:
Traditional 3
Electric 5 | Weaknesses:
Traditional 3
Electric 6 |

Opportunities:	Threats:
Traditional 2	Traditional 2
Electric 3	Electric 1

TOTAL: Strengths – Weaknesses; Opportunities – Threats	
TRADITIONAL: 3 -3 = 0 2 -2 = 0 Final Total: 0 + 0 = 0	ELECTRIC: 5 -6 = -1 3 -1 = 2 Final Total: -1 + 2 = 1
WIN: Electric car	

Here the results indicate that the electric car will be chosen due to its superior strengths and opportunities. However, sometimes this analysis can turn out to be at a tie. This can be tilted by adding extra details, such as technology, gears etc. When there is a draw between the two of them, flipping a coin might solve the problem.

This chapter proposes to give you a strategy on how to not change your mind, and you may question why I am talking about how to make a choice. Well, I am presenting this, because when you are making a calculated choice, you have less of a chance to change your mind out of the blue. People usually change their minds because they are confused about their choice, not enough information was gathered when making a choice or the choice was directed by external factors alone, which unexpectedly changed. Thus, knowing how to make the right choice is vital. Allow yourself the necessary time when making an important choice, write down the benefits and the risks in all the situations and pick the one that has the most benefits, understand that you are the one making the choice and you are the one who will live with the consequences. When you know why you made that specific choice, there will be no place for doubt or self-question. However, the method presented can be a bit slow at the beginning, but practising will make you be able to make faster, accurate decisions. Do not worry if sometimes you happened to make the wrong decision; nobody is perfect. When such a thing happens, try to remain true to yourself and make the best of your situation.

However, even if you follow the SWOT method the choice that wins might not necessarily mean that it is a perfect choice. But this choice is a well informed and thoroughly analysed choice which means that is highly unlikely to be a bad choice. By making this SWOT analyse for important choices you have fewer chances to be tempted to change your mind because you thought about your choice, and you had analysed it in detail.

VII. RELIGION and MORALITY

-why do they matter? -

There is this debate today, as to whether to follow a religion or not. Here I will not even begin to attempt to approach the metaphysics of Religion- that as per the existence of Gods and afterlife. Religion means different things to different people, and even if there is a biased belief that religious people are uneducated and have in general a below-average IQ, Religion still plays a fundamental role today. To approach the topic from an anthropological point of view is to understand how Religion evolved in line with society. From the old religions that involved costly rituals, such as human sacrifice for as little as getting rid of bad luck or causing the skies to rain to today's religions that grant absolution of sins, even murder, in exchange for repeating short prayers. Here, many would view the evolution of religions, especially religious people, or very religious people also called fanatics, that humans have degraded themselves and do not care for their souls anymore, forgetting the gods of their parents. However, from an evolutionary point of view, this is not the case. Many scholars, philosophers, anthropologists, and psychologists that follow the humanistic/existential approach, such as Marcel Gabriel, Kierkegaard, Waters, Purzycki, and many others, argue that the functions that Religion once held were overtaken by secular institutions; education and medicine once provided by monks and nuns, judiciary systems, governance, monetary services, security, and membership adherence once solely provided by the churches or temples, have been slowly and irreversibly overtaken by secular institutions such as the governments. To highlight the high fluidity a constantly growing society has is to show that even governmental institutions have been taken over by privatisation.

Religion according to Durkheim, in its basic infant form has three main functions 1) to provide group cohesion and maintain social solidarity through shared beliefs and rituals, 2) to offer meaning and purpose answering existential questions and, 3) to sustain social control and conformity by enforcing religion-based morals and norms. Durkheim stresses the importance Religion has in sustaining society, by monitoring and controlling large groups, solving existential crisis, and providing a shared identity through rituals and superstitious beliefs. Today, this function is less expressed, and because they can be easily replaced by other services or sources, Religion has become optional. Or more vulgarly expressed, therapy for the poor. However, there is one function that cannot yet be easily substituted by alternative services or institutions; this is Hope. Not the hope Snyder talks about as Snyder's theory overlaps rather with a type of locus of control than with actual hope. The rainbow, he visualised does not describe hope as it should. It rather describes a type of entrepreneurial motivation. Such as goals, ways to fulfil these goals, and inner drive. This is not hope. Scioli's attempt to define hope is better fitted. However, he may have unintentionally described Skinner's superstitious pigeon than an actual hopeful person. Scioli tried to cover too much with the hope theory, saying that hope involves one or more of these four life domains: 1) mastery, 2) attachment, 3) survival, and 4) spirituality. Scioli's error may have arisen from his fear of letting something out, as Snyder has done nine years prior. So, religion provides hope. How?

To better understand how Religion provides hope is to understand exactly what hope is. Indeed, scholars attempted to define this mysterious "thing with feathers" (Emilie Dickinson), to no avail. I will also try to break down the elements of hope. Firstly, as in the old Greek poem from Hesiod's Works and Days, hope is the last resort. Hope is the only left choice when everything seems to fail. Therefore, hope was viewed as being extrinsic, this is probably an artefact of Religion, as it associates hope with the spirituality domain as a result of faith. You must have faith in the object of your hope, be it an action, an object, a person, or a god. And according to Scioli, faith is a prerequisite of hope. However, according to Snyder hope is a more intrinsic state where the individual has faith in themselves that their effort will bring about the desired results.

This is where Religion still plays a role, as not only does Religion teaches its members to have faith, but it also teaches them that their individual efforts will bring them rewards be it in this world or the next one. Religion can provide a type of faith, however, experience can also provide faith, such as the fate that the sun will rise again tomorrow. However, hope is not just a result of faith, hope is also an emotional state *"That perches in the soul - And sings the tune without the words -And never stops - at all -"* (Emilie Dickinson). And as such, hope is a continuous state, a way of living with no expiration date as it remains for as long as the source of hope remains. Fyodor Dostoevsky nicely stated the importance of hope saying that *"to live without hope is to cease to live [at all]."*

This is one reason why Religion is still important, because is a source of hope. In turn, hope is the driving force of life, the anchor of the soul that keeps the optimistic belief alive despite any difficulties experienced. In the Collins dictionary, hope is defined as a feeling or expectation of something desirable to be true or to happen. Furthermore, Allen defined hope as an optimistic state or belief that an unknown situation will resolve in the best way for the individual, this definition is distinct from wishful thinking because it considers the surrounding reality. There is some consensus in defining hope. Still, not one definition can comprehend the complexity of what hope is. Furthermore, research hails hope as a precious medicine, thought to contribute to many positive outcomes, such as greater happiness, better career progression, higher academic achievements, and even increased longevity with more healthy years when compared to low-hope or hopeless people. In Religion, hope is a virtue, alongside faith and love. Kadlac argues that hope is a virtue because

1) It leads to a more realistic view of the future than dispositions such as optimism or pessimism, 2) Promotes courage, and 3) Encourages important social solidarity with others. Contrary to Kadlac, Mills argues that hope is better defined as a state of being rather than a virtue. A state of being originated in despair and transformed by its participation in the transcendence of the self. However, hope might be best understood if approached as a function, because 1) Is natural, innate- one does not need to learn to hope, as one learns to write, 2) It involves one or more variables and can have a variety of sources, and 3) It works and operates in a particular way to bring about results because it requires the prerequisite of faith, which can be brought about through rituals, superstitions, or talismans. From buffering the impact of hopelessness in depression and suicidal ideation to acting as a mediator for neuroticism, conscientiousness, and life satisfaction; the hope religion brings is worth noting. Notwithstanding, hope cannot exist on its own; hope is dependent on spirituality, as Scioli stated, hope requires a prerequisite of a personal faith system. Hope needs an everlasting source of faith, in such due to its long history and highly flexible nature, Religion fits this criterion.

Furthermore, Waters etches the importance of Religion for the individual and the society. Waters argues that the secular culture we live in today, which offers the freedom to deny Religion is sabotaging hope and therefore, wellbeing. He argues that removing Religion as the primary source of hope had put mistrust in our abilities to experience life. We are becoming diagnosed with ill-pathologies due to a lack of intuitive skills to experience sensations to the full. Waters paints a dark picture of the consequences of seeing Religion as optional. He argues that in ignoring the consequences of leaving Religion behind, society loses Hope, Faith, and Love. Are Waters's arguments having a bearing in everyday people's lives? There is no evidence that atheist people experience dramatic negative consequences for being non-affiliated to a religion. The most detrimental consequence identified as a side effect of not following a religion is that atheists experience discrimination and are sometimes less trusted when compared to religious people. Unfortunately, there is not enough research on Religion, because this topic has been avoided by scholars for years, not because Religion is not important enough, as every culture has some form of Religion proving that Religion is vital to people. Religion has been avoided because is a sensitive topic. Weary of discussing a topic that can produce much turmoil even today, scholars kept away from it. However, recently the topic of Religion overcame theology's constraints piquing the interest of scholars from diverse fields, such as philosophy, anthropology, history, and psychology and even medical sciences. This increased interest allowed for a better understanding of Religion, as to why it is crucial for the society and the individual, and what is the reason for its existence. However, there is a need for further analysis of the topic, as the current understanding is barely scratching the surface. Religion, as with any building block of the society, evolved, morphed, restructured, and changed direction, because as Sosis stated, Religion is an organic system. It would be irrational not to acknowledge that with the evolution of society, Religion evolved too. Religion is too interlinked with society to remain rigid and inflexible, and its presence is too widespread to ignore its importance. According to functionalist scholars, Religion has three main functions; 1) provides group cohesion and solidarity, 2) offers meaning to life through providing answers for existential questions, and 3) contributes to the sustaining of social conformity. These functions have been taken over by secular institutions during the Enlightenment. Group cohesion and monitoring, solidarity and morality exist and can be promoted without the need to belong to religious affiliations. Even the virtues that Religion and spirituality once provided seem to have been taken over by secular institutions. Faith, Love and Hope, the triad of virtues that allegedly describes Religion and spirituality, but rather applicable to specific religions, such as Christianity, Islam, Hinduism are no longer dependent on a religious or spiritual prerequisite.

The secularisation of societies, the easy access to education and the average improvement of life had morphed Religion into an optional choice. However, when everything else fails, on the brink of despair, hope pears its crowned head from the pits of doubt and failure. Hope seems to be the last remaining function of Religion, that is not too sensitive of a topic to be researched and discussed by scholars of psychology and psychiatry fields alike. Secularised institutions and other means can replace all religious functions. Just as Bloom states, societies do not require Religion to engage in prosocial behaviour, and individuals do not need a religion to be ethical, moral, and prosocial. What Religion facilitates and very often is a sole provider of when everything else fails, as a last resort, is to give hope. By answering existential questions, such as *"Why am I here (on Earth)?"*, *"What am I supposed to do with my life?"* and by providing superstitious beliefs. Giving hope does not have a deadline to meet and does not require a strict fulfilment of a request or answer but eases the mind when nothing else seems to help. Goodheart goes as far as saying that Religion may be a form of hope. The freedom to understand and investigate Religion gave rise to positive psychology from an existentialist humanistic approach with an intense focus on wellbeing. Not without reason, there is some similarity between Snyder's, Scioli's hope theory and Roger's psychotherapy approach. The humanistic approach is perhaps the one that made the most frivolous attempts to understand what works best for one's well-being. Because of the evolution of society, governments and secular institutions had taken over Religion's functions out of concern for their people's wellbeing. Now the only function of Religion that remains is hope. Some scholars are tempted to believe that this secular freedom paints a dark picture for the future of humankind, but perhaps this is not the case. Religion had carried the hard work of forming, shaping, and guiding the society into what society is today,

Religion for a long while carried the strain of being everything for its members. Today, Religion is not required to work so hard for its followers; there are other systems that can offer the support and guidance people require, with less costly sacrifices that some religions demand. A thorough investigation conducted by scholars of different fields implies that Religion may instead be a manifestation of hope. Hope transcends the limits of an emotion or a state, because of this it is better described as a function. Is hope the last remaining function of Religion? I really hope that is not the case. Religion still has much to offer; I doubt that hope is the only function Religion has. However, the limited research available to answer this question makes it look like hope is the last remaining function of Religion, especially in secularised societies. Perhaps this is where Religion is heading. At the bottom of the box, deep into the darkness, hope sat last of them all in Pandora's box. Tight kept in unbreakable prison, the only light left in despair.

Why am I presenting you such a long debate on Religion and religious beliefs? Because, understanding how religion works helps us respect all religions and the personal choice of the people who follow a religion different to ours, who are atheists, or who purely do not hold any religious views. Furthermore, in the darkest of times the only string that keeps us from succumbing into the darkness it might be the sliver of hope religious beliefs bring. Just like the famous mathematician, Pascal said, one should rather risk believing in God even if God does not exist because in the end if God does not exist, he loses nothing and if God does exist, he wins everything.

The takeout from this long debate is that religion is the cornerstone of the modern society as we know it. It gave birth to a moral, prosocial, well-constructed society where its members collaborate for the wellbeing of the group. Religion was a great thing, and in underdeveloped countries is still very important. One should have respect for what Religion made way to, regardless of their theistic beliefs. However, Religion has bad sides too, it is like a sword with two sides, one good, and one eaten by rust. Religion gave rise to many wars, historically known as crusades, killed many bright scientists under the excuse that they may be working with the devil, and cursed many individuals by suppressing minorities and opposite religions under the pretence that the outside members are impure. Religion was, and still is in some societies the weapon of those in power. This can clearly be seen from how and where Religion facilitated the expansion of great ancient empires, such as Egypt, where the pharaohs were gods. However, the birth of religions and the fear of punishment delivered by supernatural gods gave birth to morality. Although, many pro-nature scholars, such as Paul Bloom, argues that morality is innate, rather than socially learned, a rich body of research tends to disagree with these findings. Furthermore, Maslow argued that humans are good in nature, however, this is not necessarily the case. Yes, we do inherit certain behavioural and personality traits, but we are more influenced by the environment and our personal choices than by genetics when it comes to social behaviour. If it happens that the child resembles its parent behaviour, is not because of the blood that runs in their veins, is because "monkey see, monkey does"; and their behaviour reflects what they learnt from their parent. Human babies, despite their low physical abilities, learn incredibly fast because adapting to their environment means surviving. If the social environment is prosocial and shows fairness and morality, even if the baby will not be able to engage in the behaviour, the baby will understand it and will be able to judge according to which agent can harm them, and which will protect them. Therefore, morality is not innate. Morality is a socially learned behaviour.

Does one need to be religious to be moral? No, if they are part of a secularised society, they do not need to be religious to be moral, they might automatically end up being moral due to their environment, such as a pro-social education, laws, displays of charitable actions, etc. However, if they are born in an underdeveloped society, and do not belong to a religion, their survival instincts might not naturally guide them towards morality and pro-sociability, even more so if they can avoid judicial punishment. Their behaviour might instead be governed by a survival instinct where the strongest has more power.

Thus, Religion is important because it can meet two fundamental functions for the survival of an individual as part of society; it provides hope, and it facilitates morality. For such functions, one should acknowledge and respect Religion regardless of their religious views.

VIII. MANAGING STRESS

There is almost no human being on Earth who does not experience stress at least once in their entire life that also believes that stress is bad and should be avoided at all costs. But, au contraire, stress is not bad, is not something to be afraid of, and most certainly not something to suppress. Although this may come as a surprise to many, stress is in fact, an aiding mechanism. People are often mistaking the onset of stress as something terribly toxic, and yes, they are right to a certain degree, but also very wrong. When we experience stress, our hearts begin to beat faster, our breathing rate increases and the blood flow changes course, focusing on feeding the skeletal muscles and the brain, leaving little to the visceral organs. But this is a good thing; because it prepares the organism to fight or fly. The increased breathing rate is providing more oxygen to the brain, and the increased heart rate is pumping more blood throughout the organism. However, in a society where fighting or running away from the situation might not be the best outcome the instinctual way to deal with these responses is to inhibit them. Sweating is a result of inhibiting the primary instinct of fight or flight and trembling a result of the adrenaline rush.

To deal with stress in a 'modern' way is to firstly acknowledge that stress is not a damaging negative thing. Firstly, stress appears when we take risks and when we search for meaning in what we're doing. Researchers believe that stress appears when the arousal level of an individual is higher than the arousal level that the action requires. Secondly, stress is a guiding emotion in satisfaction, researchers believe that stress plays an important role in reaching an optimal level of arousal, or how Csikszentmihalyi called it, a state of flow. A state where the skills that an individual possess are matching the skills required to perform a certain task. When there is an imbalance between the two parties, boredom or stress may appear because of the imbalance produced by engaging in the task with unmatched skills. Thirdly, stress increases the breathing rate and by pumps more blood, in turn reducing reaction time reduces, and the chance for making errors is minimised, making us ready to perform at an optimal level.

Recent research at Stanford University found that the participants who believed that stress is not damaging but is aiding them in performing at an optimal level have experienced no negative effects and performed better than the group of participants who believed that stress is damaging to their health and performance; these participants have performed worse than sub-optimal and have also experienced negative side effects such as palpitations and excessive sweating. Indeed, there is a form of stress that is highly toxic. This stress is called chronic stress and is a direct result of sleep deprivation. Chronic stress can often lead to ischemic strokes, vascular diseases and even heart infarcts, being linked to six leading causes of death. Unfortunately, occasional stress can also lead to chronic stress, The secret roots in how we approach stress; like any other situation, our minds can turn a specific opportunity into a dream or a nightmare, becoming self-fulfilling on its own. Therefore, people who believe stress is damaging and even deadly will make that prediction self-fulfilling, but people who approach stress with an optimistic mind, will make the most of stress and instead of considering stress their enemy, they will make it their friends.

To identify if stress is becoming an issue for you, follow the below checklist. Do you have these symptoms?

THOUGHTS	
I must get this done	
I'll never finish	

There is too much to do, and too little time	
It's not fair. Someone should be helping me.	
This is too much - I can't cope!	

Although these examples are generic, the thoughts that occupies a stressed mind are navigating around these main topics, of overwhelmingness, unfairness, and endlessness.

EMOTIONS	
Irritability	
Anger	
Impatience	
Anxiety	
Hopelessness	
Sadness/Depression	

From an emotional point of view, too much stress can disbalance a person making them feel the worst they ever felt, and this expands into making the people around them feel bad too. In many cases, excess stress begins to affect the individual's mental and physical health.

PHYSICAL	
Heart racing, pounding	
Breathing faster	
Tense muscles; neck, shoulders,	
Hot, sweaty	
Difficulties concentrating	
Headaches	
Forgetful	
Agitated	
Bladder or bowel problems	

The physical response to stress is caused by the body's adrenaline response - the body's alarm signal and survival mechanism when faced with a perceived threat.

BEHAVIOUR	
Sleep disturbances	
Unable to settle	
Continuous rushing	
Shouting, arguing about the smallest things	
Eating more or less than usual	
Drinking more alcohol than usual	
Using illicit drugs	
Smoking (more than usual)	
Crying more often or more easily	

The above symptoms of stress are what gets in the way of living life well, living life happily. Fortunately, stress is not permanent, it can be managed and even turned into something we can benefit from. *What is the secret to making stress your friend? Is it avoiding stress? Is suppressing it? Is it masking it?* No. None of these. The secret is to embrace stress. Stress is what gives meaning to our lives, and meaning is what makes us happy. Planning for exams, for getting into a new job, for a presentation, for any kind of event is half the work on how to perform optimally while under stressful situations. The second part of the work is anticipating the result of failing or succeeding after going through that specific stressful situation. Very often we put a lot at stake in taking a decision, and we believe that failure will mean even the end of our lives. We weigh too much in the outcome of certain situations, and that is what increases the level of stress we experience. Here stress may better be represented by fear or maybe even phobia. This is why, a stressful situation can lead to panic attacks and even heart failures. We are the worst judge of ourselves, but to deal with stress, we must understand that failing is a possible option. As with anything, how we chose to visualise something is how we will react to that something; is choice over matter, where the mind has all the control. Chose to not be affected by stress and your mind will follow suit.

Now, talking about planning. Planning is essential in managing stress, because planning reduces the chances of forgetting, becoming overwhelmed, or running out of time. Plan the tasks you have and accord the necessary time to do them. And even more importantly, plan wind-down time. Be it an hour each day, a weekend away, or a short relaxing holiday before beginning a major project. Having a planned time for winding down can work wonders on your well-being. When I was in university, before every semester's final exam, I would start revising early and then take a break for a few days before the session - usually less than a week- to reduce the stress that accumulated. Other people choose to have a spa day or a nice aromatherapy massage before or immediately after dealing with a stressful situation, think about the party the people are enjoying right before getting married, the purpose of that party is not to have the last chance on doing any type of deed that could be questioned in a marriage, the purpose of that party is to allow the marrying couple to clear their minds and make sure that the answer they give in front of the altar is their best choice. Well, that doesn't work that well when intoxicated thou'.

Now, how to deal with stress? Firstly, know that you're only human, and surely you are not the only person who feels stress. Secondly, accept yourself, accept your weaknesses and understand them. Understanding yourself is knowing how you will react in a certain situation and anticipating anything that could negatively influence your optimal functioning. Are you bad on an empty stomach when giving a presentation? Then make sure you have something to eat before the presentation. Are you nervous when talking to many people? Well, who isn't? But there are tricks for that too, for some people imagining the audience in their underwear releases the pressure they feel, for others, imagining that the audience is just their big family, works, for others, closing their eyes and imagining that there is no one else in the hall with them, works. And there are many other tips and tricks famous people use; you can inspire yourself from them. Others have a specific ritual before going through a specific stressful situation. Others are practising until the task becomes their second nature and rely on automatization when in stressful situations.

I recall my reaction when I had my first job interview, I was shaking like a leaf, my voice trembling, words barely coming out of my mouth, my mind unfocused, even my eyesight blurred. And that was also happening each time I would give a group presentation in front of the class. But I learned that drinking a cup of coffee before a presentation or an interview helped me react better under stressful situations. Also, to combat this awful anxious reaction that I would experience at an interview, I started to apply for random jobs that I was not planning to take, and I was not anxious about the result. That was my way of gaining experience with interviewers. I have also observed that the less I would have to gain from succeeding through a stressful situation, the less stress I would experience. When I know that my chances to succeed are small, I am telling myself that failing would only make me lose my time and that I can always try again or, if I could not try again, I would comfort myself by saying that at least I satisfied my curiosity and if I had not tried, I would not have known how going through that specific situation made me feel, or what the results would have been.

In conclusion, to make the best of a stressful situation is to firstly learn to realistically anticipate the result so you can be prepared for the "unexpected", and secondly is to plan or practice the process of the stressful situation. Try to embrace stress as a friend and accept that losing is a possible option, and most importantly always have a plan B. Below is a list of little tips that can make a great difference in reducing the level of stress we encounter in our daily life.

+ When you must be somewhere, start getting ready hours before. Better be 2 hours earlier than miss the train by half a minute.
+ Prepare for the morning the night before.

+ Set appointments ahead and keep them in a calendar or an agenda.

+ Do not rely on your memory- write it down.

+ Even the simple act of writing down can aid memory recall.

+Say "no" more often. You do not have to accept everything and do everything leaving no time for you to breathe.

+Set priorities straight in your life, keep goals for yourself. Is best to do this at the beginning of each new year. Write a letter to yourself with what you would like to achieve during the year and re-read the letter verifying the goals you managed to achieve.

+Always make copies of important papers. This one goes without saying, best to keep these copies in a digital format, somewhere where you can access them from anywhere, such as Drive or Cloud.

+Ask for help, some people love helping others, do not be afraid to ask for help, even from strangers.

+Break large tasks into bite-size portions

+Look at problems as challenging games that you can have fun while solving them.

+Be prepared for rain; this can extend to other similar events that can come unexpectedly but are not unusual, such as losing your house key, or your card etc.

+Play with a pet or even a plush toy. This may sound a bit strange, but soft touch is therapeutic.

+Say something nice to someone, complimenting someone else, making someone else smile helps us feel better about ourselves.

+Engage in random chatting with a stranger.

+Do something new.

+Buy yourself flowers or something that you like. Have you heard of shopping therapy? Is real, shopping somehow helps people release their stress and feel better.

+Keep a diary. Keeping a diary is not only a way of remembering what happened during the day or how we felt. Keeping a diary is like talking to someone who fully understands you, who will not judge and will listen to you no matter what time of day or how long you are talking because a diary is a way of communicating with yourself.

+Remember yourself; just take time for yourself to be with yourself and listen to yourself only.

+Allow yourself to be childish from time to time, give the child what belongs to the child.

+Go for a walk in the nature, exercise.

+Listen to music, it's therapeutic.

+Eat healthily.

Here is a quick questionnaire to evaluate your level of stress. Look at each of the questions and answer yes or no to see how much stress you might be experiencing at this current moment.

Do you have trouble sleeping?	
Do you feel exhausted?	
Do you feel run down?	
Do you suffer from headaches?	
Do you have periodic shortness of breath?	
Have you had significant weight loss/gain?	
Do you suffer from irritability and anger?	
Do you have mood swings?	
Do you become easily frustrated?	
Do you have indigestion or abdominal discomfort?	
Do you feel an increased mistrust of others?	
Do you feel vulnerable or helpless?	
Has your work efficiency declined?	
Have you lost interest in others socially?	
Has your work productivity declined?	
Have you become far too critical, or negative of others?	
Do you feel you are losing control?	

Are you often nervous or scared?	
Do you find your problem solving is more rigid?	
Do you have trouble relaxing?	
Are you accident-prone?	
Do you feel guilty?	
Do you lack enthusiasm for being alive?	
Do you have poor concentration?	
Do you have frequent colds, flu etc.?	
Do you have increased work/school absences?	
Do you have increased alcohol/drug use?	
Do you have poor time management?	
Are you afraid of the worst happening?	
Do you have reduced self-worth?	

If you answered yes to all the questions, or to more than 25 questions, please call your GP as soon as possible and discuss how they can help you with reducing stress. You can also try to contact local/national mental health organisations such as Mind or the Talking Space because if stress has such a widespread existence in your life the next immediate stages are depression and suicidal ideations. If you answered yes to less than 25 questions, I still advise you to contact your GP and discuss how stress affects you and how this can be minimised. If you answered yes to less than 20, just try to make the changes and implement the tips I mentioned earlier, make yourself your priority. These simple changes should be enough to help you return to a harmonic inner state. If you answered yes to less than 10 questions, stress is not a problem for you, and the symptoms might stem from something else, such as not sleeping enough the night before, hormone imbalance, or just the result of skipping a meal.

IX. HUMAN RELATIONSHIPS

Not to sound too dogmatic but treating others how you want to be treated is how you effectively make good friends. Aristotle said that we are social animals, being social is in our nature, therefore making friends should not be a problem we encounter. Despite that, there are still people struggling to make friends, or who engage in toxic relationships. Others have experienced bad relationships, and that is preventing them from trusting people again. I will firstly discuss the nature of trust, which is the first of the building blocks for any relationship. Secondly, I will discuss communication which is the essential ingredient in any sort of human interaction.

What is trust? Well, trust is a complex term better represented on a gradient scale. Trust varies from person to person, from interaction to interaction, from situation to situation and from time of day or time of year to time of day and time of year. Let us picture this in more detail: Let's say is June, past midnight and a person dressed up as a Santa Claus walks behind you in a dark alley ringing a bell and asking you if you've been naughty or nice. I am not sure what you would do, but I am absolutely sure that I will run as fast as I can. But take the same man with the same words and change the time of the year to December, the time of the day to midday, and the location to the middle of a mall and the level of trust increases significantly, you might even smile and wave at the Santa, and even let your children take pictures with the Santa dressed person. Furthermore, any of us is more likely to trust someone close, like a friend or family member or a person in authority than a stranger. Even more importantly is with what we trust people, we are more likely to trust someone we don't really know with small things, like letting us know what time of day is, or if the X number bus is delayed, but we will most certainly not trust the same person with the keys of our home or our children.

Secondly, about communication. Without communication, any human interaction would be pointless. Like trust, communication can also be described on a gradient scale, from brief facial expressions communication to written and spoken language. However, this is not the type of communication I am referring to. I am referring to communication as a way of exchanging personal information that is real and accurate with the purpose to know more about each other and interact effectively. Communication and trust are a sort of currency between people, a currency that cannot be weighted or stored in a wallet, but a currency that has an even greater value. Like any currency, in a relationship, people would have to first accumulate this currency before asking for the right to spend it. To build this currency, at first people will be kind, will do favours, be polite, listen and only later in the relationship, when there is enough currency accumulated, favours can be asked. So, to gain trust and communicate better, you will have to make the first step. There are many people who say that they build trust between people and that they do not trust people from the beginning. Here most of them are making a mistake, to build an effective relationship, you must first give trust to the other person. However, this trust is indeed built, but not from nothing, it is built from small amounts, if the trust has not been violated, it will increase. Same with communication, at first partners, would exchange small innocent personal information, if the information exchanged has been successfully received, and the level of trust increased, more information would be exchanged in a mutual relationship. Those are the basis of any sort of relationship, be it romantic, business, casual, or even familial relationships. Trust and communication begin small and grow at a steady rate. However, it can happen that these terms may be violated and with these, a break usually occurs, if the cause of the break can be identified and fixed, the trust and communication between partners can be re-built. This is the basic process of making friends.

How exactly does one make friends? Making friends can happen naturally because of social interactions and because "Birds of a feather, flock together". Thus, people who share similar interests are more likely to become friends, and more likely to have a strong bond. However, this is not the golden rule. People can just become friends because they feel like they "clicked" or because they simply feel good being together. Feeling good together is usually the core element of any partnership. In conclusion, if you're looking to make friends learn to be the first to approach the potential "candidates" and focus on the group of people who share the same interests as you. For example, if you enjoy classical music, searching for friends at the rock music festival might be absurd- unless you also like rock music. An effective approach for people to increase the circle of their friends is to join a community, through short courses, volunteering, or attending a church.

Another critical aspect to friendships is keeping the friends you make. Keeping a friendship is like ensuring the tree you planted stays alive. In some circumstances, the tree grows simply due to the rain and sun it receives, but sometimes this tree needs to be watered and fed nutrients. As such it is very important to at least remember the friends' birthdays and other important celebrations, such weddings or baby showers. Also, make sure that you send a card or make a phone call for Christmas, Easter, Eid, and other major annual celebrations they might follow. It is also important to make time to see them if that is convenient for the both of you. Making friends and keeping friends should not be difficult and should happen naturally. However, due to the life we live in now, and especially during the COVID pandemic, this process has slowed down and even stagnated. Humans need face to face interactions to create a successful relationship, but what humans need above anything else is, to be honest with each other; this is the safest and fastest way to creating true and long-lasting relationships. The list below describes a few ways of finding compatible friends.

+Go study- be it a short course or a whole degree; this is a safe way of making life-long friends.
+Go volunteer for a cause you care about; this is a great way of making friends who have the same believes as you do.
+Go work for a big employer; the more people, the more chances to find compatible friends.
+Go out more often- be it in pubs, clubs, restaurants, or parks; you need put yourself in the public eye to be seen.
+Go join a social club, gym membership, or even a worshipping community; you must spend time with others to know others.
+Go be the first to introduce yourself at work, events, out in the public (if the situation is appropriate for this).
+Go be present at networking events from your university, neighbourhood, or work.

X. LOW MOODS

There are times when we might feel low, might feel unhappy and overall sad. These feelings are perfectly normal and are part of experiencing life, these feelings usually appear because of negative life events or by the absence of something that made us happy in the past, or we perceived as having the potential to make us happy. No matter how happy a person may appear to be, we all experience sadness from time to time. Sometimes feeling low is a sign of a serious illness, but most of the time is a reaction to an unhappy event in our lives. It would be irrational to smile and be cheerful when we experience a serious loss of something material or emotional. Sadness and unhappiness are part of a healthy life if the emotional response is rational, natural and has an obvious cause. If feeling low does not seem to have an obvious cause, it happens suddenly, is intense and lasts for a long time, please do not hesitate to see a doctor as soon as possible. It does not have to be a psychiatrist or a psychologist; seeing your family doctor may very often be enough.

Failing a promotion, an exam, losing customers, breaking up with your partner, can make one feel worthless and reconsider their self-esteem. The first step to take is to understand that losses are natural and happen because of being alive. The second step is to rationalise the cause of the loss and evaluate what went wrong, and what can be learnt from the experience. The third step is to understand that the past cannot be changed and therefore, the focus must be on making a shift in the present moment-*what can be done to improve your current situation?* The fourth step is to rid yourself of the stress and the negative feelings that appeared as a reaction to the unhappy event. The fifth step is to remember that only by failing, we succeed, and that pain is a way of learning (see table below).

<table>
<tr><td>

UNDERSTAND- Understand that misfortune is part of life and is a normal human feeling.

RATIONALISE THE PAST- Try to explain to yourself (or others) what happened but do not ruminate into the past longer than necessary.

FOCUS ON THE PRESENT- Do not cherish the past for too long, look at what opportunities the present brings you so you can turn them into successes soon.

CLEAR THE NEGATIVE EMOTIONS/ MEMORIES- Memories paired by emotions last for a lifetime, and those that hurt last even longer, yet we cannot erase memories at choice.

</td></tr>
</table>

However, we can always make new memories. When the hurting memories seem to flood everything try to change them into more positive ones by changing the perspective, the light we see them on. Sometimes asking the question; what we learned from those memories helps repurpose hurtful memories. Sometimes making new memories with one of the hurtful aspects from the hurtful memory can help recondition how we feel about the memory itself. Such as creating a good memory in the place where something bad happened. These are just a few methods that can help return to the equilibrium state.

REMEMBER TO LEARN- Learn from previous experiences and make new memories.

Now, you might say that I am giving you Freudian psychoanalytical advice that conceals and defends against the negative feelings, and you will be half right. Throughout history, humankind created defence mechanisms embedded within the society; one such is the belief in a set destiny that an individual is meant to go through. Such belief is widespread and wears many suits such as horoscope, karma, and even Religion. For example, the pain of losing someone dear is very often healed by religious rituals which are designed to set the soul of the deceased at peace, but truly these rituals are designed to set at peace the mind of the people left behind. Because *"death does not happen to the deceased, it happens to everyone around [them]"* ("Teen Wolf"-the series). Also, the existence of Heaven and Hell, Destiny, Luck and Karma are attenuating the pain that is felt when something bad happens to us. Freud simply put it as projecting the blame on someone or something else, but hey, it works! However, this method still allows if not even encouraging intense rumination which is deeply harmful to the individual.

In contrast, rationalising what happened is different from rumination. Rumination is a mental rehearsal of what happens which only makes the event even more painful because rehearsing the event is forever etching it into the long-term memory. One should avoid rehearsing the event at any cost, however rationalising the event/events is helpful, but only when being completely objective and calm about what happened. Take the event and imagine that it happened to someone else, someone that is not you, and is not even a close friend of yourself. Imagine that the event happened to a stranger, this stranger is telling you what happened to them and is asking for your advice. This is also known as illeism, which according to a large number of ancient scholars might make you become wiser. The extreme of this 'method' is known as depersonalization disorder, but a pinch of depersonalization applied to the right situation at the right time is healthy, even helpful.

But the most important aspect of dealing with any time of distressing event is understanding, understand that you are only human (see song-"Human" by rag'n'bone man), not a superhero. Humans have limited strengths and are prone to mistakes. Ridding yourself of the stress and negative emotional charge that surfaced because of experiencing this unhappy event is extremely important. It is not recommended to engage in unhealthy behaviours, such as consuming excessive amounts of alcohol, trying illicit drugs or smoking, although these may help and may seem effective, they cause more harm than help. Instead, a chocolate bar may be better than that. However, food or drinks are not an effective way of dealing with low moods either, because they only affect the chemical concentration for a short period of time, the best way of dealing with low moods and unhappiness is by creating new positive memories, because memories remain with us for a long time. Arguably, for those patients suffering from Amnesia or Alzheimer some memories translate into feelings, and even if they can no longer access these memories, they can still access the feelings of these memories. The stronger the new happy or at least neutral memory the more effective treatment it becomes, in such, seeing a comedy movie or reading jokes will be less effective than going out with friends or learning a new productive skill. The most efficient way in dealing with unhappiness is to use a counterbalancing gradient scale. Just how black will have as opposite white, so losing a friend will have as opposite gaining a friend. However, some events become tricky to counterbalance, either because it does not have a clear counterbalancing match, it is impossible to achieve, or because it might cause more harm than help. In the beginning, the counterbalancing match should be made by neutral activities, such as those that create a state of relaxation. Nevertheless, one should keep in mind that many of the events that create these negative feelings can be resolved; a bad job can be replaced with a better one, lack of skills can be replaced by learning, and lack of money can be replaced with earning money. Although these may seem as having a simple solution, getting to the contempt, happy feeling is very often a complex process; it involves not only understanding the situation, removing or counterbalancing the emotional charge, and finding a rational solution, it also involves being ready for the change. This readiness can only be assessed by the individual; it cannot be forced; however, it can be advanced using a self-directed technique, such as self-praise, self-complimenting, and making positive self-comments. These self-directed techniques work even better when are done by the individual in front of a mirror. As such I have created the Stress Counterbalancing Equalizer for Negative Events or SCENE for short. Although this 'equalizer' is on a beta status, it had been developed from practical work with clients dealing with difficult events. The SCENE table gives solution method appropriate for some of the most common difficult events according to Holmes and Rahe stress scale.

Stress Counterbalancing Equalizer for Negative Events (SCENE)	
Death of spouse	Lone time for self-reflection, activities done in the name of the spouse, honouring the spouse's wishes, gaining a new family member or/and godfathering/godmothering.

Divorce	Dating, meeting new people, new relationship, self-discovery.
Marital separation	Focusing on self (self-discovery), Lone time, celebration of appropriate.
Jail term	After jail term- travelling, doing charitable work. During jail term- focusing on self-improvement.
Death of close family member	Activities done in the name of the deceased individual, honouring their wishes, gaining a new family member.
Personal injury or illness	Focusing on self-reflection, improving self-care.
Marriage	Now this depends on the type of marriage and if it was out of love or convenience. The direct counterbalancing would be divorce or separation which applies if the marriage was unwanted by any of the partners. Alternatively, the counterbalancing action is celebration and communication.

Fired at work	New job, new course, retirement.
Marital reconciliation	Communication, making time for lone self-reflection, and taking part in activities that are of interest for both spouses.
Retirement	Taking a part time job, joining a hobby, travelling, or volunteering, celebrating.
Change in health of family member	Taking time for self, increasing self-care.
Pregnancy	Planning and preparing, celebrating if appropriate.
Sex difficulties	Focusing on psychological and physical general health.
Gain of new family member	Planning and preparing, taking lone time for self-reflection.

Business readjustment	Lone time for self-reflection, taking time off, appreciating the things you have.
Change in financial state	Lone time for self-reflection, planning, appreciating the good things you have.
Death of close friend	Doing activities in the name of the friend, honouring their wishes, making new friends.
Change to a different line of work	Lone time for self-reflection, focusing on professional improvement, taking time off.
Change in number of arguments with spouse	Communication, appreciating the good memories you have together.
A large mortgage or loan.	Reducing spending, increasing income, learning better budgeting.
Foreclosure of mortgage or loan	Declaring bankruptcy, revising budget.

Change in responsibilities at work	Communication, focus on self and professional improvement.
Son or daughter leaving home	Hosting events at home, increasing circle of friends, returning to hobbies, communicating with the child.
Trouble with in-laws.	Communication, lone time for self-reflection.
Outstanding personal achievement	Appreciating the things, you have received, being thankful, celebrating successes.
Spouse begins or stops work	Communication, planning, sharing responsibilities.
Begin or end school/college	Being thankful, celebrating
Change in living conditions	Lone time for self-reflection, appreciating the things you have.

Revision of personal habits	Lone time for self-reflection, communication, focusing on self-improvement.
Trouble with boss	Communication, changing bosses/jobs.
Change in work hours or conditions	Lone time for self-reflection, communication, negotiating alteration to work hours or conditions if unhappy with the change.
Change in residence	Housewarming party, lone time for self-reflection, joining local communities, meeting local people.
Change in school/college	Celebrating if appropriate, meeting classmates, getting involved in school/college's activities/events.
Change in recreation	Lone time for self- reflection and self-evaluation.
Change in church activities	Lone time for self-reflection, communication, planning.
Change in social activities	Lone time for self-reflection, communication, planning.

A moderate loan or mortgage	Revising of budget.
Change in sleeping habits	Consulting with health professionals.
Change in number of family get-togethers	Communication, planning, lone time for self-reflection.
Change in eating habits	Consulting with health professionals.
Vacation	Lone time, self-time.
Christmas	Planning.
Minor violations of the law	Self-reflection.

XI. DEPRESSION

Depression is one of the most common mental health problems in the whole modern civilization with 1 in 6 people suffering it at some point in their life (Mind, UK), and that was before the COVID pandemic begun. There is no clear line between everyday depression and clinical depression because like any other feeling, depression falls on a gradient measured in units of intensity. When depression is more severe, more long-lasting, and more widespread in its effects then it might be the case that the person feeling depressed needs specialist help. However, in this type of situations depressions is often accompanied by other symptoms, described below.

+Depressed mood- Feeling low, sad, fed-up, or bleak, numb, and empty. Sometimes, depression can progress into illeism or anhedonia. Illeism meaning a complete dissociation from self with an inclination of seeing self as being someone else, and anhedonia meaning a complete lack of pleasure, even from activities that were previously perceived as pleasurable.

+Losing interest, enjoyment, and motivation- Nothing seems like fun anymore, everything feels like a 'must do'. Life and existence seem grey, boring, and pointless.

+Self-criticism and guilt- Feeling that you are bad, useless, inadequate, or worthless.

+Increased irritability and unexplained anger.

+Pessimism- Seeing the most negative interpretation of everything that happens.

Thinking that there is no way out, that nothing will ever work out right ever again. Generally, seeing the world through dark glasses.

+Hopelessness- Thinking that things will always be negative, dark, bleak, and pointless and that the future will only bring further misery and loss.

+Feeling anxious- Feeling worried or tense, often without knowing why.

+A general loss of energy that can't be replenished.

+Reduced activity- This might reach the point where people just lie in bed or sit in a chair all day without doing anything.

+Finding it hard to be with people- Finding it draining, irritating, or pointless to talk to people and intentionally withdrawing from social activities.

+Being either excessively restless, agitated, and fidgety; or the extreme opposite; doing everything much more slowly than usual.

+Difficulty in concentrating- Often to the point where it is difficult to follow a piece of written text, a TV programme, or a conversation.

+Memory difficulties- For example forgetting where you have put something down, inability to recall people's names, or finding it much easier to recall the bad memories.

+Changes in sleep pattern- Sleeping too much or too little.

+Changes in appetite and weight- Most often a loss of appetite and weight, but sometimes people might 'comfort eat', resulting in weight gain.

+Loss of interest in sex.

+Though of death- These thoughts might range from thinking it would not be bad to be killed accidentally, to actively making plans for suicide. In medical terms this is called having "suicidal ideations".

Clinical depression, however, is not the same as everyday low mood or feeling a little bit depressed. Mental health practitioners use a list of symptoms including depressed mood, loss of pleasure, weight changes, sleep changes, being agitated or slowed down, loss of energy, feeling of worthlessness, concentration difficulties, and thoughts of death or suicide. The professionals are diagnosing this change of mood as a 'major depressive episode' only when five or more of these symptoms are present most of the day, nearly every day, and for a continuous period of at least two weeks. In addition, these symptoms must cause the sufferer significant distress or impairment in their day-to-day life. Fortunately, depression does eventually go away even without treatment. However, for some people depression is a recurrent problem. This is because up to half of the people who have one depressive episode will go on to have another one at some time in their lives. This may seem alarming, but there is evidence that with medication and continuous psychological treatment it is less likely to have a reoccurring episode, and if that happens it is less likely to be as intense as the previous one. Therefore, treatment does help. Treatment not only contributes to speed recovery but can also significantly reduce the likelihood of having another depressive episode in the future.

The reasons why people become depressed are thought to be comprised of both biological and psychological factors. The biological factors are related to the hereditary sensitivity of the neurochemical receptors we are born with. Such that, a child whose parent had depression is more likely to suffer from depression at some point in their life. However, this biological tendency to become depressed acts like a gene marker dependent on the environmental factors also termed psychological factors. These psychological factors include adverse life events early in life, exposure to continuous stress, and lack of social support. A hereditary sensitivity to depression paired with negative psychological factors is more likely to trigger depression in an individual comparative to hereditary sensitivity alone. Due to the intertwining of the biological and psychological factors responsible for triggering depression, the most effective treatment is one that targets both aspects by prescribing anti-depressive medication and cognitive behavioural therapy. The anti-depressive medication can be prescribed by the individual's GP after having a mental health assessment and at the same time, the psychiatric nurse who makes the assessment will also refer the person for psychological therapy. Cognitive Behavioural Therapy, Problem- solving therapy, Interpersonal Psychotherapy, and other less common therapies, such as keeping a thought diary, positive mirror talks, regular physical exercise, and mindfulness, are employed in treating depression either on their own or combined.

<u>WARNING:</u> IF YOU FEEL DEPRESSED, PLEASE CONTACT ANY OF THE FOLLOWING:

SUPPORTLINE:
Helpline: 01708 765200
Email: info@supportline.org.uk

YOUNG MINDS:
Text YM to 85258, free from EE, O2, Vodafone, 3, Virgin Mobile, BT Mobile, GiffGaff, Tesco Mobile and Telecom Plus.

THE SAMARITANS:
Free phone: 116 123
Email: jo@samaritans.org
write them a letter, or visit them at one of their 201 local branches

MIND:
MindInfoline: 0300 123 3393
Website: mind.org.uk
CHILDLINE:
Helpline: 0800 1111
Website: childline.org.uk

PAPYRUS:
Hopelineuk: 0800 068 4141
Website: papyrus-uk.org

XII. CBT

One cannot talk about self-improvement without mentioning CBT. CBT stands for Cognitive Behavioural Therapy which is a type of therapy based on two main ideas; the way one feels based on thoughts/beliefs (cognitions), and actions (behaviour). Although this definition might seem simple, CBT is designed to reflect the complexity of human behaviour as influenced by others, by past experiences, perceived future, and set expectations. CBT works by focussing on changing the individual's inner perception of the world, for such, the focus of the CBT is rooted in thoughts, which then are reflected in behaviour. Because depression is one of the most common mental health disorders the human species suffers from. I will shortly summarise the CBT model of depression- see Managing Depression booklet by David Westbrook for a more in-depth approach.

The CBT model has several stages. Firstly, it suggests that vulnerability to depression arises from beliefs about self or others learnt in early childhood. For example, a child who was abused might learn to believe that they deserved the abuse, that they are bad or unlovable, this belief is often developed as a coping mechanism. However, some beliefs may not be strong enough to cause immediate problems. But later in life these beliefs might activate and intensify when encountering negative situations. These beliefs then grow creating negative thoughts which in turn feed into depression. Once the negative thoughts become automated, the negative beliefs are reinforced and are progressively affecting the individual's mood. After a while, these negative thoughts become indisputable truths in turn affecting the individual's behaviour. At this stage, depression is settled in a vicious inescapable circle. Luckily, there is a way to escape the vicious circle of depression. CBT is a technique that puts the self in the centre, and it can be used even as self-help without losing its effectiveness. Below are described a few of the techniques which can be practised fighting against depression.

Schedule your time.

If our mind is not occupied with something else, negative thoughts can take over it. By keeping active these negative thoughts, we are denying ourselves power over our minds. For such, every waking moment of our day should be filled in by activities, which after completing should be evaluated in terms of Achievement and Pleasure. These terms are used to fight against the two most overwhelming symptoms of depression, lack of pleasure, and lack of achievement. Use A(Achievement) and P(Pleasure) to evaluate the activity and give it numbers, this could be from 0 to 5, or from 0 to 10. Use this method for several days to steer away from spending your days curled under the blankets in an anhedonia state.

Time	Monday	Tuesday
07:00	Got up, took a shower PO A6	
8 AM	Had breakfast P1 A7	
9 AM	Went for a walk outside P3 A5	

The above table is just an example and should be tailored to yourself as much as possible. Alternatively, this activity table can be replaced with a "to-do" list/diary prepared the night before or early in the morning. When you have completed the record for at least a week, look back and see what you can learn from it. There are three main things to look for, activity, achievement, and pleasure levels. By observing your trends, you can notice where you should focus your resources.

Check your activity levels

Measure which activities are scoring the highest, see what adjustments you need to make. After reviewing the records see how you can improve your activity level and the sense of achievement. You might have learnt that spending more time in nature is scoring higher than any other activity. Or perhaps, being creative seems to be the winning type of activity. This type of record can teach you which path to take out of depression.

Identify negative thoughts

Negative thoughts play a central role in keeping the individual in a low mood. To tackle the low moods, one must fight the negative thoughts. The first step, like in any war is to "know the enemy", to fight back effectively you must understand in detail what your individual pattern of negative thoughts is. This type of record is like the activity record. Below is a partially completed example.

Date and Time	Situation	Emotion severity (0-100)	Thought Belief (0-100)

4/04 08:35	Missing the train	Anxiety (80) Disappointment (60) Angriness (80)	"I can't even be in time for the train" (80%) "I am useless" (80%) "I am unreliable" (60%)
5/04 01:25	Can't sleep	Angriness (60) Sadness (80)	"Why can't I just fall asleep like normal people?" (100%) "I am useless, I can't even sleep when I need to sleep." (25%)

In the beginning spotting the negative thoughts is difficult, so do not blame yourself for not being able to spot these thoughts straight away. Even for people who are not suffering from depression filtering their thoughts is a challenge that requires practice and tuning. Here is an exercise recommended by Dr Daniel Wendler:

https://www.improveyoursocialskills.com/, this exercise asks you to focus on your emotions. As you go through your day, keep an eye on your emotions, and look for times in which you are feeling something, whether positive or negative, then take time to think why you are feeling that way. Go below the surface, it's easy to have someone cut you off in traffic and say "Well, I feel angry because I was cut off." But if you go deeper, you might realise that your angriness has a deeper cause, you might feel angry because the other driver disrespected you, and you don't feel respected in your relationship. Or you might feel angry because you're hurting from a hard time that you are going through, but you are not acknowledging the pain. You might even realise that you don't have a valid reason to be angry, and as a result, your anger will fade away.

Fight back with distractions

Earlier in this booklet, I had made a point in saying that distractors are harmful. Well, I am not taking my words back now, but against depression distractors are a sharp weapon. Here, distractors are used to stir away from negative thoughts. By doing other things to occupy the mind there is less space for negative thoughts. These distractors can be activities such as going for a walk, reading a book, or even binge-watching a TV show. Other depression suffering people came up with much simpler methods to tackle negative thoughts, such as counting all the green objects around them, reciting poems in their mind, and even praying. Anything that is perceived by you as being pleasant, funny, and can help you keep your mind busy can be used to fight against these thoughts. Distractions is a good short-term method but is not a cure for depression.

Thought challenging

A better method for fighting against negative thoughts is to challenge them. The aim of the thought challenging technique is to bring your negative thoughts under the limelight and look at them with a magnifying glass. Very often the negative thoughts we have are misleading and are distorting reality. If you find them to be inaccurate the first step is to correct them. It is important to understand that though correcting is not the same as positive thinking, however, seeing every situation as positive may be more realistic than seeing everything as negative. To engage in thought challenging, you must first write the thought down and think of various ways of challenging this negative thought. Sometimes, getting someone to help you can accelerate this process. You should ask the following questions when challenging negative thoughts.

<u>Are there signs of thinking errors?</u>

Overgeneralising, black-and-white thinking (thinking in extremes), emotional reasoning (turning feeling into facts), fortune-telling (assuming the future will be in a certain way), or mind-reading (assuming you know what other people think). These are all thinking errors and should be challenged as soon as they are noticed.

<u>What is the evidence behind these thoughts?</u>
<u>What are the pros and cons?</u>

These questions refer to what grounds the thoughts are built upon and what are the advantages or/and disadvantages of keeping these thoughts. By answering these questions, we should know which viewpoint to assume regarding the specific negative thought.

<u>How is the negative thought affecting my behaviour?</u>

Lastly, mind over body. Test out how different thoughts affect your behaviour, observe how your behaviour differs when acting against the negative thoughts. For example, for the thought "They are going to hate my presentation." act by following the thought "They are going to love my presentation". Observe how your behaviour is affected just by changing your attitude or your perspective.

Problem Solving

Another very effective method of fighting against depression is employing the problem-solving technique. This method invites you to focus on finding solutions for the practical problems you might be struggling with. Follow these steps to problem-solving:

1. Identify the problem you want to work on,
2. Think of as many possible ways of solving this problem- write down anything that comes into your mind as a possible solution,
3. Select the best possible solutions,
4. Evaluate the pros and cons for the selected solution(s),
5. Break down in 'baby steps' the process needed to reach the solution,
6. Put into action the process by taking one step at a time,
7. After initiating the first step, review how it went,

8. Continue the process until the problem is solved, or until it becomes clear that the solution is unbefitting. If that happens, restart the process.

Problem solving is not only a proactive method that can keep the individual busy and fight against negative thoughts, but it can also destroy the root of depression itself. As such, many organisations that have at its centre any type of rehabilitation employs a problem-solving plan for the individual. In this way the solution gives autonomy and creates motivation for change conveniently supplying self-actualisation.

Now, I have given you weapons, dress yourself with all of them and fight from the deepest corners of your heart against the invisible enemies of your life that stand to steal the happiness, peace, and blissfulness like a con-master that tricks its ways into your life day by day. Fight them, and cast them into the unknown, never to return.

RECOMMENDED READING

American Psychiatric Association. *Diagnostic and Statistical Manual of Mental Disorders. Fourth Edition*. Washington, DC: American Psychiatric Association, 2000.

Berne, E. (1964). *Games people play*. USA: Grove Press.

Burns, D (1980). *Feeling good*. New York, NY: Avon Books.

Buttler, G. & Hope, T. (1995). *Manage your mind*. Oxford, UK: Oxford University Press.

Department of Health. (2005). *Mental Capacity Act*. London, UK: HMSO.

Dickinson, E. (2011). *Hope is the Thing with Feathers* (254). Academy of American Poets.

Gilbert, P. (1997). *Overcoming depression*. London, UK: Robinson.

Maslow, A. H. (1943). A theory of human motivation. *Psychological Review, 50*(4), 370–396. https://doi.org/10.1037/h0054346

Participation, E. (2018). *Equality Act 2010*. Legislation. gov. uk, available at:

https://www.legislation.gov.uk/ukpga/201
0/15/contents [accessed 19 October 2020]

Ryan, R. M., & Deci, E. L. (2000). Self-determination theory and the facilitation of intrinsic motivation, social development, and well-being. *American psychologist, 55*(1), 68.

Rotter, Julian B (1966). Generalized expectancies for internal versus external control of reinforcement. *Psychological Monographs: General and Applied, 80*, 1–28. doi:10.1037/h0092976.

Scioli, A., Ricci, M., Nyugen, T., & Scioli, E. R. (2011). Hope: Its nature and measurement, *Psychology of Religion and Spirituality, 3*(2), 78.

Snyder, C. R. (2002). Hope theory: Rainbows in mind. *Psychological Inquiry, 13*(4), 249-275.

United Kingdom: Human Rights Act 1998 [United Kingdom of Great Britain and Northern Ireland], 9 November 1998, available at: https://www.refworld.org/docid/3ae6b5a7 a.html [accessed 19 October 2020]

Wendler, Daniel (2021). *Improve your Social Skills*, available at:

<u>https://www.improveyoursocialskills.com/</u>
[accessed: 09/09/2021]
Westbrook, D. (1999). *Managing Depression.* Oxford, UK: Oxford University Press.

Guides for mental health and wellbeing services available in the UK

Seeking help is not a sign of weakness, is a sign of courage.

BEAT: <u>https://www.beateatingdisorders.org.uk/</u>
CITIZENS ADVICE:
<u>https://www.citizensadvice.org.uk/benefits/universal-credit/claiming/helptoclaim/?gclid=Cj0KCQjw_8mHBhClARIsABfFgpgerRCh6GxDHeCOW1M2lSVEy83WU0_0fAHLJ6I9qZu5ahwvKv1Nvu0aAtUuEALw_wcB</u>
LGBT+: <u>https://www.tht.org.uk/hiv-and-sexual-health/sexual-health/trans-people/resources</u>
MIND: <u>https://www.mind.org.uk/media-a/2900/seeking-help-for-a-mental-health-problem-2017.pdf</u>
NHS: <u>https://www.nhs.uk/mental-health/talking-therapies-medicine-treatments/talking-therapies-and-counselling/nhs-talking-therapies/</u>

RESTORE: https://www.restore.org.uk/about-restore

TED:https://www.ted.com/talks?sort=relevance&q=wellbeing

THE BRIDGE: https://www.thebridge-uk.org/?gclid=Cj0KCQjw_8mHBhClARIsABfFgpiQctWB2LAeVIQTqwm2iGsB72YlWi6jykMyd83YC_KRh3ay0JaaeeoaAq8bEALw_wcB

TURNING POINT: https://www.turning-point.co.uk/services.html

WAVELENGHT:https://wavelength.org.uk/what-we-do/?gclid=Cj0KCQjw_8mHBhClARIsABfFgphSw5f6wK8std9E6QJe8bBUIYzZvZwo2UECn9zBkIhNChWMXe2Dtk0aAmOtEALw_wcB

YOUNGMINDS:https://youngminds.org.uk/find-help/

The best way of knowing yourself is to be true to yourself. Listen to that inner voice, don't easily dismiss it.

THOUGHT DIARY

Date/Time			
Situation			
Thought Belief (0-100)			
Emotion severity (0-100)			

THOUGHT DIARY

Date/Time			
Situation			
Thought Belief (0-100)			
Emotion severity (0-100)			

THOUGHT DIARY

Date/Time			
Situation			
Thought Belief (0-100)			
Emotion severity (0-100)			

FIGHTING STRATEGIES DIARY date __/__/____		
Thoughts	**Feelings**	**Fighting Strategies**
Example: I am sick of working so hard and not getting any results.	I feel disappointed, I feel like I want to give up. I feel tired.	Take a "me" break. Understand that results take time. Learn to appreciate and celebrate small successes.

FIGHTING STRATEGIES DIARY date__/__/____		
Thoughts	**Feelings**	**Fighting Strategies**

FIGHTING STRATEGIES DIARY date__/__/____		
Thoughts	**Feelings**	**Fighting Strategies**

FIGHTING STRATEGIES DIARY date__ / __ / ____		
Thoughts	**Feelings**	**Fighting Strategies**

<table>
<tr><td colspan="3" align="center">FIGHTING STRATEGIES DIARY date__/__/____</td></tr>
<tr><td>Thoughts</td><td>Feelings</td><td>Fighting Strategies</td></tr>
<tr><td>

</td><td></td><td></td></tr>
<tr><td>

</td><td></td><td></td></tr>
<tr><td>

</td><td></td><td></td></tr>
</table>

TO DO LIST date:__/__/______

TO DO LIST date:___/___/________

Learn to listen to yourself...